YOU ARE IN CONTROL

TOUGH *Financial* CHOICES

OZZIE **TORRES**
STEPHANIE **TORRES**

Copyright © 2023 by Ozzie & Stephanie Torres

All rights reserved. No part of this publication may be reproduced, stored, or transmitted in any form or by any means, electronic, mechanical, photocopying, recording, scanning, or otherwise without written permission from the publisher. It is illegal to copy this book, post it to a website, or distribute it by any other means without permission.

First edition

This book was professionally typeset on Reedsy. Design elements were created on Canva. Printed by Amazon.

A Note From
STEPH & OZZIE

Who is this book for?

You! Whether you're stuck in the financial mud and don't know how to get out of your situation, or you are ready to grow your wealth, this book is for you. You might be feeling like, "Now what?" and we are here to help you learn how to make the solid choices that can propel you toward the life you desire for yourself and your family.

Why should you read it?

Here's the thing - it's easy to feel like you've already tried every strategy out there for improving your financial well-being and achieving your dreams. But nothing seems to stick. We believe that it starts not with knowing everything there is to know about finance, but with a foundation of practicing how to make thoughtful, educated choices, one at a time.

What about us?

That said, we are not financial advisors, accountants, or attorneys. We have learned a lot through our personal financial journey and talking to many others at various of stages in their lives. We will share more about our story as we go along because we believe learning from your experiences and others' is key to growth. Professionally, we own a real estate company called Contigo Real Estate in Lancaster, PA. Stephanie is a PA Real Estate Broker and we are both licensed Realtors®. Ozzie has his MBA, which has equipped him for leadership in our business and community.

Why did we write this?

We have talked to countless friends, family members, and clients who are frustrated with their financial limitations and feel like there is no way out, while having a deep desire to be able to reach their dreams for themselves and their families. We want to be able to share with you the same conversations that we have with them. We see this book as if we are sitting down for coffee and walking you through the steps to financial recovery, stability, and success, one choice at a time. Our heart is to see that you become filled with hope and confidence in your own ability to improve your situations. You have big dreams and you CAN achieve them. Let's go!

TABLE OF CONTENTS

10-18
INTRODUCTION

19-43
CHAPTER 1
FACING THE REALITY OF YOUR SITUATION

44-62
CHAPTER 2
EXPLORING YOUR OPTIONS & MAKING A PLAN

63-104
CHAPTER 3
THE CHOICE MAP

105-111
CHAPTER 4
RUNNING OUT OF ROOM

112-118
CHAPTER 5
MAKE THE CHOICE

119-123
CHAPTER 6
FINANCIAL CHALLENGE: THIS OR THAT

Introduction

Welcome to Tough Financial Choices, the book that will help you overcome your money challenges and improve your financial health. This book is for anyone who is facing difficult or stressful financial decisions, such as how to pay off debt, how to save for retirement, how to buy a home, how to deal with a divorce, and so on. These decisions can have a huge impact on your life, not only financially, but also mentally and emotionally. That's why we wrote this book: to help you make the best choices for your situation and future.

In this book, you will learn:

- ❖ How to face the reality of your situation & accept your financial challenges

- ❖ How to explore your options and strategies & make a plan of action

- ❖ How to overcome the obstacles and challenges that may arise along the way

- ❖ How to celebrate your progress and achievements & accept your choices

❖ How to anticipate the next choice & learn from your experience

We will guide you through each step with practical tips, examples, and stories from people who have been through what you're going through. We will also provide you with resources and tools that you can use to further improve your financial situation.

This book is not a magic formula or a quick fix. It is a process that requires honesty, openness, willingness, and action. It is also a process that can be rewarding, empowering, and fulfilling. By following this book, you will not only make tough financial choices, but also improve your financial health and well-being.

In this book, we challenge you to identify your financial goals - whether they are big or small, short- or long-term - and commit to taking daily actions that will help you get there.

We encourage you to take the time to reflect on your current financial situation, your priorities, and your values.

What do you want to achieve?
What kind of life do you want to live?
What kind of legacy do you want to leave behind?

Once you have identified your goals, we challenge you to create a plan of action and stick to it. This plan may include saving a certain amount of money each month, cutting back on unnecessary expenses, or seeking additional sources of income.

The key is to start small and make consistent progress. Remember that every small decision you make has the potential to have a big impact on your financial future.

Throughout this book, we will provide you with practical tips and strategies to help you make tough financial choices that align with your goals and values. We will also share inspiring stories of individuals who have faced similar challenges and have come out on top.

We want you to understand that this book applies to all stages and goals whether you're saving to pay off a credit card, buying a new car or home, or saving to retire. Your daily choices affect your progress.

Are you ready to take on the challenge and start making tough financial choices that will change your life for the better?

WHAT MOTIVATES YOU?

Pick your two goals.

SHORT TERM:

LONG TERM:

Before we hop into the first chapter, let me tell you two stories:

Story One

There was a young couple who had just gotten married. They had high hopes for their future together, but they were starting out with very little. They couldn't afford much, so they rented a small basement apartment. They ate the cheapest food they could find, often having hot dogs and chips for lunch daily. They drove old cheap cars that barely worked, and they worked long, hard hours at physically demanding jobs that left them in pain at the end of every day.

The couple knew they needed to make changes in their lives, but they felt trapped. They had no direction and no clear plan for their future. They felt lost and hopeless, knowing that they could be stuck in this situation for years to come.

Despite their struggles, they tried to stay positive and find joy in the little things. They spent their evenings watching old movies and reading books from the library. They took long walks in the park and enjoyed picnics on sunny days. They talked about their dreams and plans for the future, hoping that someday things would get better.

But as the days turned into weeks and the weeks turned into months, the couple began to feel more and more discouraged. They saw their friends and coworkers living in beautiful homes with new cars, enjoying expensive recreational activities, eating at nice restaurants, and taking fancy vacations. They couldn't help but feel envious and embarrassed when they couldn't participate in the same activities. They wondered if they would ever be able to afford the same luxuries, even sketching out a drawing of their dream home that they wished they could have one day.

As the years passed, the couple's situation did not improve much. They still lived in the same basement apartment, still ate cheap food, and still drove old cars. They had managed to save a little money, but it was not enough to make a significant difference in their lives. Poor choices led them to spend money on things that added momentary satisfaction to their lives.

Story Two

There was another husband and wife whose situation felt suffocating. They were drowning in debt and it seemed like every paycheck was already spent before it even hit their bank accounts. They had both grown up hearing about the American Dream - a big house, a fancy car, and a comfortable lifestyle. They thought that getting an education and buying two cars was the way to achieve that dream, but now they realized that it came at a steep cost.

Their school loans were massive, and the monthly payments on their cars were draining their bank accounts. Not only that, but they bought a home that was over their budget, maxing out the amount the bank told them they qualified for out of an emotional decision to buy the pretty house on the block. They tried to cut back on expenses, but it seemed like everything was a necessity. They didn't want to admit it, but they felt trapped. The weight of their financial burden was heavy, and the thought of losing their freedom because of it was terrifying.

They had seen family members lose their homes and their possessions due to financial struggles, and they didn't want to end up in that same situation. The fear of losing everything they had worked for was constantly looming over them. They didn't know what to do or where to turn to obtain a sense of financial security.

The couple tried to stay positive, but they couldn't shake off the feeling that they had made a grave mistake by buying into the American Dream. They realized that what they thought was the path to success was actually the path to debt and instability. They wished they could go back in time and make different choices, but it was too late.

As they lay in bed at night, they would often talk about their situation and what they could do to get out of it. They knew it wouldn't be easy, but they also knew that they couldn't continue living like this.

They needed to find a way to break free from their financial burden and start over.

How can you make choices when things seem like there aren't any options left? Are you ready to start? Let's begin with chapter one: Facing the reality of your situation.

Small choices made daily can lead to big goals achieved over time. Take the challenge to discover your financial aspirations and pave the path to a brighter future.

Chapter 1
Facing the Reality of Your Situation

We get it. You've hit a hard time, had to pay for hospital bills with a credit card, and then were given a pay cut at work. Then Christmas hit and you wanted to provide your kids with a magical Christmas morning, so you added more onto the card. When summer rolled around, your siblings decided to go on vacation together with their families and before you knew it, you opened a second credit card and loaded it up with Disney passes, flights, and hotel charges. You've worked hard this year and you didn't get to spend as much time as you would've liked with your kids, so when they ask for the princess experiences and superhero costumes, how are you going to say no? Your kids had the time of their lives, so the sweat, exhaustion, and meltdowns were worth it, right?

Sitting in the airport between flights back home, you scroll your phone and you see your Realtor® friend posted yet another photo congratulating their clients on buying their first home. Your gut sinks, remembering the phone call you had with the mortgage lender last fall. He said you needed to raise your credit by paying off those credit card bills, and to save up for closing costs if you wanted to be able to buy a house. You've made the minimum payments, but life happened and you wanted to give your family a great experience. How do you choose between making memories, being present with your kids on vacation and providing a stable home for your family to grow up in?

You turn off your phone and sigh, feeling defeated. Looking at your kids playing next to you on the terminal bench, you wonder if there's a way to move forward without them having to sacrifice. How do people do it?

Does this sound familiar?

Let's start with the basics. If you want to make tough financial choices the right way, you need to face the reality of your situation. That means being honest and realistic about the money problems you have, and how they affect your life. It may not be fun or easy, but it is necessary if you want to get out of the limitations of your current situation and move forward.

We know it's hard to be honest and realistic about your financial challenges, because sometimes it may feel more comfortable to hide from or avoid them. Unfortunately, when we do that, we lie to ourselves, pretending that everything is fine when it really grows worse and worse underneath the surface. The consequences must ultimately unveil themselves if not dealt with. That often happens at the most inopportune times: when the bank account is already close to or below zero, your health puts you at risk of hospitalization, your company goes through layoffs and you're taking the cut, etc.

Financial challenges can be overwhelming and stressful, but it's important to face the reality of your situation. Ignoring or denying financial issues can lead to more significant problems down the road. Accepting and acknowledging the financial challenges you're facing is the first step towards finding a solution.

Denial or avoidance may seem like an easy way out, but it can make things worse in the long run. When you ignore financial problems, they can quickly escalate, and you may find yourself in a worse situation than you were before. Acknowledging the issue may be difficult, but it's the first step towards a brighter financial future.

We have talked to many people who have never written out their income and expenses to create a budget. The main challenge with never setting up a budget is that money comes in and goes out without ever really having a grasp on where it's being spent. It can seem so easy to make the decision between whether to stop at the drive through or wait until you get home and make dinner yourself. You're tired, it's been a long day, and you just want to eat quickly and relax, so you pull into the drive through and pay with the card, barely batting an eye at the total. The cost isn't as high as a sit-down restaurant, so you figure it's the cheaper option and doesn't really hurt anything.

The challenge comes when those quick purchases add up without noticing. Eating out, adding a couple extra things to the cart at the grocery store or Target, signing up for another TV subscription because they just moved your favorite show - again... All of those under $11.99 purchases can go unnoticed if you're not looking at them closely. When someone takes the time to look at and categorize their expenses, it can immediately hit home how much is being spent and which spending is unnecessary. We've all spent more than we should have, so please understand that we are not blaming anyone for overspending. The important takeaway here is that we can't make progress and grow without first observing what got us to where we are now.

Avoiding your financial weaknesses can make things worse by messing up your view of reality. If you hide or avoid your money problems, you may not see clearly how things are right now. You may not know how much money you owe, how much money you make, how much money you spend, and so on. You may also have wrong ideas or guesses about how things will be in the future. You may think that it will take forever to pay off your debt, that you will never have enough money to retire, that someone else will bail you out, and so on. By messing up your view of reality, you may make poor decisions that can hurt your financial situation even further without even realizing it.

Another way that avoiding self-confrontation can make things worse is by hurting your mental and emotional health. If you hide from your money problems, you may not deal with the feelings and thoughts that they cause. You may feel fear, worry, sadness, guilt, shame, anger, frustration, and so on. These feelings and thoughts can affect how you function throughout all aspects of your life. They can also affect how you get along with others. You may have trouble with your family, friends, partners, co-workers, and so on. By hurting your mental and emotional health, you may lose the ability to handle stress and enjoy life.

But don't worry. We're here to help you be honest and realistic about your money problems. Here are three tips to keep in mind as you begin this journey:

Be Truthful with Yourself

You need to admit to yourself that you have a problem and that you need help. Don't try to make excuses or blame others or things outside of your control. Don't try to make your problem seem smaller or bigger than it is by comparing yourself to others or using extreme words. Be fair and objective about where you are and where you want to be.

Be Open with Others

You need to tell others about your problem and ask for help from people who care about you and want the best for you. Don't be ashamed or embarrassed to ask for help from people who can support you and help you. Don't be too stubborn to listen to feedback or advice from people who know what they're talking about or have been through what you're going through. Be respectful and thankful for their help and advice.

Be Ready to Change

You need to accept that you need to change some things in your life in order to solve your money problems. Don't fight or refuse the changes that are needed or that are good for your financial improvement. Don't stick to old habits or ways that are bad or useless for your financial situation. Be flexible and ready to try new things and opportunities.

Being honest and realistic about your money challenges is not a sign of being weak or a loser. It's what makes you strong and brave. It's the first step towards making tough financial choices that can make your situation and future brighter.

We know it's not easy to face the reality of your situation. But we believe in you and we're here for you. You can do this!

Change is not easy,
but it is necessary for growth.
Embrace it, take the leap,
and watch yourself soar
to new heights.

Common Financial Problems and Their Impact

Financial problems come in various forms and can have a significant impact on your mental and emotional health. Some of the most common financial problems include:

Debt

Debt can pile up quickly, and it can be challenging to pay off. Living paycheck to paycheck can be stressful, and the fear of not being able to make ends meet can be overwhelming. It also hurts a lot less handing over the credit card to pay for everyday expenses than seeing the money being withdrawn from your bank account. While there may be an immediate comfort of being able to pay with a credit card, it creates a false sense of security, making yourself believe you're in a better situation than you actually are. When you do have to confront the debt or struggle to pay it back, it can cause a lot of stress and anxiety. Credit scores drop, creditors come calling, and you're left in a situation where you feel stuck, overwhelmed, and unsure how to get out.

Josh & Amanda were a young couple who had just moved to a new city. They were excited to start their lives together and wanted to furnish their apartment. Amanda had been scrolling Pinterest for months planning out the design of their home, imagining furniture and decor they didn't currently have. Josh loved cooking and entertaining their friends, so he had developed a desire for high-end appliances and technology in the kitchen. The challenge was that they unfortunately did not have much savings available as they had both just graduated college.

They went to a rent-to-own store, where they found a beautiful sofa, accent chair, dining table & chairs, a big-screen TV, and a stainless steel refrigerator, as well as a few new kitchen gadgets promising ease of entertaining. The salesperson assured them that the payments were affordable, and they could own all of these items in no time. The couple signed up without reading the fine print or understanding the high interest rates and hidden fees. They were thrilled to bring home and set up all of their new things. However, their jobs weren't quite stable yet after college and they failed to create a budget to outline their income and expenses.

Soon, Josh & Amanda started falling behind on their payments. They had taken on more than they could handle, and their bills were piling up. One day, they came home to find a debt collector from the rent-to-own store waiting for them. They were scared and didn't know what to do. The debt collector threatened them with legal action and damage to their credit scores if they didn't pay up immediately.

The couple felt trapped and helpless. They had become attached to the possessions they didn't even own yet, and they didn't want to lose them. They worked extra hours, took on odd jobs, and cut back on essentials like food and utilities just to make their payments. They even borrowed money from family and friends, causing strain on their relationships.

The stress and anxiety of the situation were taking a toll on their mental and physical health. They couldn't enjoy their new city or their new life together. They regretted their decision to sign up to rent-to-own their possessions without fully understanding the consequences, instead of just buying what they could afford.

In the end, Josh & Amanda paid off their debt over time, but at what cost? They had sacrificed their well-being, their relationships, and their financial stability for possessions that didn't even belong to them. Paying much more for these items than they would have if they had saved up and bought them with cash, they learned a valuable lesson about the importance of patience, financial education and making informed decisions.

Unemployment
Losing your job can be one of the most challenging situations to face. Not only does it cause financial stress, but it can also impact your emotional well-being and sense of self-worth. Whether it's short-term or long-term unemployment, the consequences can be severe and far-reaching. Sadly, if you don't have a job or a source of income, it can cause serious feelings of depression and hopelessness.

For example, consider the story of John. John had worked at a large corporation for over a decade, but due to company downsizing, he was suddenly let go without warning. At first, John was optimistic that he would find a new job quickly, but after months of searching without any success, he began to feel hopeless and defeated. The stress of not being able to pay his bills was mounting, and he found himself feeling depressed and anxious. He started to lose his sense of purpose and identity, feeling like he had lost his place in the world. Initially, John expected to be able to find a position in the same field he was previously working in. He applied to many jobs and even attended several interviews, but he still had not received calls back. As time went on, he applied to positions that were more and more removed from what he was previously doing. He felt defeated as he had been confident in his career path before. He was humiliated that he could not maintain his previous career and way of life.

John's friends were mostly from work and related to his industry. As time grew from when they had seen him at work, the distance also grew in their relationships until he was no longer invited to happy hour or dinners. John felt like his life was slipping away from him. But eventually, it became more and more apparent to him that he needed to broaden his search to positions outside of his previous experience. He applied to jobs he previously had thought beneath him, but John was surprised to find that he connected well in an interview for a position he would have never considered before. He was offered and accepted the job, albeit at lower pay, but over time John was pleased to find more enjoyment in that position than he had in the high-pressure environment he was in before his lay-off.

Changing his expectations and opening up his options was the biggest turning point in John's life toward a better future.

Unemployment not only affects one's financial stability, but it can also have a severe impact on mental health. The feelings of sadness, hopelessness, and low self-esteem are common, and it's crucial to address them. Staying connected with friends and family, reaching out to support groups, and seeking professional help can be helpful in maintaining a healthy mindset. It's also important to focus on your skills and strengths and to find ways to continue developing them, whether through volunteering or taking online courses.

While it's easy to feel isolated while being unemployed, it's important to remember that you're not alone. Many people go through similar experiences, and there are resources available to help you get through this difficult time. By taking care of your mental and emotional well-being and focusing on personal growth, you can come out of this challenging experience stronger and more resilient than ever.

Medical Bills
Medical bills can be expensive, and unexpected medical emergencies can quickly add up. Medical bills can be unexpected or unavoidable, depending on whether you have insurance or not, whether you have an emergency or a chronic condition, whether you have preventive care or not, etc. But if you must pay for medical bills that you can't afford or that are not covered by your insurance, it can cause a lot of

anger and frustration. Coping with medical bills can be emotionally draining and overwhelming. You may feel angry, irritated, annoyed, or resentful. You may blame yourself or others for your health situation. You may also feel frustrated by the lack of options or solutions for your medical problem.

Divorce

Divorce can be expensive, emotionally draining, and can cause significant financial stress. Splitting assets and dealing with legal fees can be overwhelming and stressful. You may feel worried about how to cope with the changes in your finances (income, expenses, assets, liabilities, etc.), and insecure about your financial future. There are life-changing decisions to make like whether to sell your house, where you will live, and how to live on a single income. It is important to seek out the expertise of others to help guide you through this process like a trusted attorney and real estate advisor.

These are just some examples of major life situations that can wreak havoc on your financial situation. There are of course many other financial challenges that you may face in your life, such as losing a home, starting a business, retiring, etc. Each of these financial problems can have a significant impact on your mental and emotional health. Financial stress can lead to depression, anxiety, and other mental health issues. It's important to recognize the impact that financial challenges can have on your overall well-being and seek help if needed.

Please know that you are not alone in your financial challenges. Here's the thing: there's not a magic one-size-fits-all formula to address all situations. I bet you know that by now. If there was, you probably would have Googled and found it, and be rockin' and rollin' through your care-free life. Instead, every single one of us needs to figure out how to navigate all the options in life available to us to make the best choices with what we have right now.

So, you've had your challenges, your opportunities, and, for better or for worse, you've recognized where you're at currently. Here's what we can do now: Let's take a look at the different types of tough financial choices that we encounter and walk through a Choice Map of what we can do with each of these situations. The goal is to be able to better handle the choices that come up so we can gradually redirect our life toward the outcome that we want to see.

CHOICES

Forced Choices

Poor Choices

Smart Choices

3 Types of Financial Choices:
Forced, Poor, & Smart Choices

Forced Choices
Before deciding what kind of choice you are going to make, it's crucial that you evaluate whether the choice in front of you is absolutely necessary to make or not. Decisions can often feel much more pressing than they actually are, so take a step back and observe. Is this a forced choice that you have to address or are you putting this pressure on yourself based on societal or peer pressures?

Poor Choices
Poor financial choices are those that can lead to more significant financial challenges in the future. For example, taking on unnecessary debt, spending money frivolously, or failing to save for the future can all be poor financial choices. These choices may provide short-term satisfaction, but they can lead to long-term financial stress.

Smart Choices
Smart financial choices are those that can help you improve your financial situation. For example, creating a budget, paying off debt, or investing in your education can all be smart financial choices. These choices may require some sacrifice in the short term, but they can lead to long-term financial stability and success.

Let's take a closer look at each of these three types of financial choices to better understand how they impact our lives.

Forced Choices

When facing financial challenges, you may feel like you're being forced to make certain decisions. Yes, some situations are unavoidable and have to be addressed. But it is crucial when evaluating a decision that you take a step back and recognize whether you absolutely must make this choice or if it is voluntary.

Let's say you're facing a financial challenge where you need to come up with a large sum of money quickly. You may feel like your only option is to borrow from a payday lender, even though you know the interest rates are high and it could put you in a worse financial situation down the road.

In the immediacy of the moment, it may feel like you're being forced to take this option because you don't see any other way to come up with the money. But if you take a step back and evaluate the situation, you may realize that there are other choices available to you, such as asking for help from friends or family, selling some items you no longer need, or even taking on a part-time job.

By recognizing that this choice is actually voluntary, you can make a more informed decision and avoid getting trapped in a cycle of debt and financial insecurity. If you do realize that the choice is optional and not as urgent as it may initially seem, it can actually take a lot of pressure out of how you choose to move forward. This can instantly relieve the amount of stress on your shoulders, allowing you to then make a smart choice.

Forced financial choices are those that you have no control over. For example, if you lose your job, you may be forced to live on a tighter budget, change your living situation, or find a new job quickly. These decisions can be challenging, but it's important to recognize if they are outside of your control.

Another example of a forced financial choice is an unexpected medical emergency. If you or a loved one is faced with a serious health issue, you may be forced to spend a significant amount of money on medical bills, leaving you with little choice but to find ways to cover the cost. This could involve dipping into your savings, taking out loans, or even selling assets to pay for medical expenses.

When faced with forced financial choices, it's important to remember that these situations are often out of our control. While we may not be able to control the situation itself, we can control how we respond to it. This means being prepared for unexpected events by building an emergency fund and having a plan in place for how to handle sudden changes in our financial situation. It's important to understand that no matter what we will be faced with forced decisions at some point in our lives. The more we can be prepared, the more we are setting ourselves up for success so that we can make smart choices when the time comes.

Once you evaluate if a choice is absolutely necessary or not, then you can move forward with the appropriate amount of urgency into making a smart decision over a poor decision. Of course, the choice you make will have a significant impact on your future outcomes, whether you're limiting yourself or providing optimal future opportunities.

Poor Choices

Poor financial choices are those that can lead to more significant financial challenges in the future. These choices may provide short-term satisfaction or relief, but they can have long-term consequences that impact our financial health. One example of a poor financial choice is taking on unnecessary debt. This could include using credit cards to pay for non-essential items or taking out loans for purchases that we can't afford.

Spending money frivolously is another example of a poor financial choice. This could include buying items that we don't really need or overspending on things like entertainment or dining out. While these choices may provide some immediate gratification, they can quickly add up and leave us with less money to cover essential expenses like rent or bills.

Failing to save for the future is also a common poor financial choice. Without a savings plan, we may be caught off guard by unexpected expenses or changes in our financial situation. This can lead to relying on credit cards or loans to cover expenses, which can create a cycle of debt and financial stress.

It is important to understand that even though you may have made poor choices in the past, you're not done being able to improve your life. We strongly believe that you are not stuck by your past circumstances. You may feel limited in your current situation, but there is always a way to improve and grow, even if it is little by very little. We will walk you through this.

Smart Choices

Smart financial choices are those that can help us improve our financial situation over time. These choices often require some sacrifice in the short term, but they can lead to long-term financial stability and success. One example of a smart financial choice is creating a budget. By setting a budget and sticking to it, we can gain a better understanding of where our money is going and identify areas where we can cut back on expenses.

Another smart financial choice is paying off debt. Debt can be a significant burden on our finances, as it often comes with high interest rates and fees. By making a plan to pay off our debt, we can save money on interest and fees and improve our credit score over time.

Investing in our education is another example of a smart financial choice. By pursuing higher education or skills training, we can increase our earning potential and open up new career opportunities. This can lead to higher income and greater financial stability over the long term.

Here it is! This is why you're reading this book, right? I think I'm safe to guess that you saw the title and thought something along the lines of, "Hey, I'd like to learn how to make better choices to improve X, Y, or Z in my life." Am I right? Then, great! In Chapter 3, we will outline for you our Choice Map. Our hope is that this will be a resource for you as a guide to evaluate your options when you encounter obstacles in life to work through. The goal is that you will put these steps into practice time and time again so that you become so highly skilled at making tough choices that they become easier and easier, and your life moves in the direction of your dreams!

In summary, understanding the different types of financial choices can help us make better decisions and improve our financial health over time. By recognizing the impact of forced, poor, and smart financial choices, we can take steps to prepare for unexpected events, make wise investments in our future, and avoid unnecessary financial stress.

It's essential to recognize the difference between forced, poor, and smart financial choices and how they can impact your future outcomes. Making smart financial choices can help you achieve financial stability and success in the future. It all happens one small choice at a time, gaining momentum and strength in your choice-making muscles so that you can make great decisions when the tough financial choices arise.

Evaluating Short-term and Long-term Consequences

It's essential to understand how the choices you make today can impact your financial future. Evaluating the short-term and long-term consequences of your decisions is critical in achieving financial stability. For example, choosing to buy a new car instead of saving for a down payment on a home may provide short-term satisfaction but could impact your ability to purchase a home in the future. Instead, you could use the $3,000 you have now to buy a car with cash that can at least get you from Point A to Point B. By doing this, you could save the hundreds of dollars per month toward your home purchase that would have been spent on a car loan. Not to mention, you'll save on the high auto loan interest rates and avoid owing more on the car than it's worth as the value of the car depreciates. In the long run, you'll be much happier that you set yourself up for success in achieving your goals by making one smart choice.

It's important to remember that taking responsibility for your financial situation is not the same as blaming yourself for everything that has gone wrong. Life can be unpredictable, and there are often factors beyond our control that contribute to our financial challenges. However, by accepting responsibility for your situation, you can take back control and start taking steps towards a better financial future.

One way to start taking responsibility is to stop making excuses. It's easy to fall into the trap of thinking that your financial problems are someone else's fault, or that you don't have the time, energy, or resources to make changes. But the truth is that nobody is going to solve your problems for you, and making excuses only prolongs your suffering. Instead, try to focus on what you can control. Make a list of your financial goals and the steps you can take to achieve them. Start small if you need to and celebrate your successes along the way. By taking proactive steps towards a better financial future, you can break the cycle of victimhood and start building a life you can be proud of.

In summary, the first step toward overcoming financial challenges is to acknowledge and accept the reality of your situation. By facing your problems head-on, you can start making smart financial choices and take control of your future. Remember that making mistakes is part of the learning process, and that nobody is perfect. The key is to learn from your mistakes, take responsibility for your situation, and take proactive steps towards a better financial future.

WHERE IS YOUR MONEY GOING?

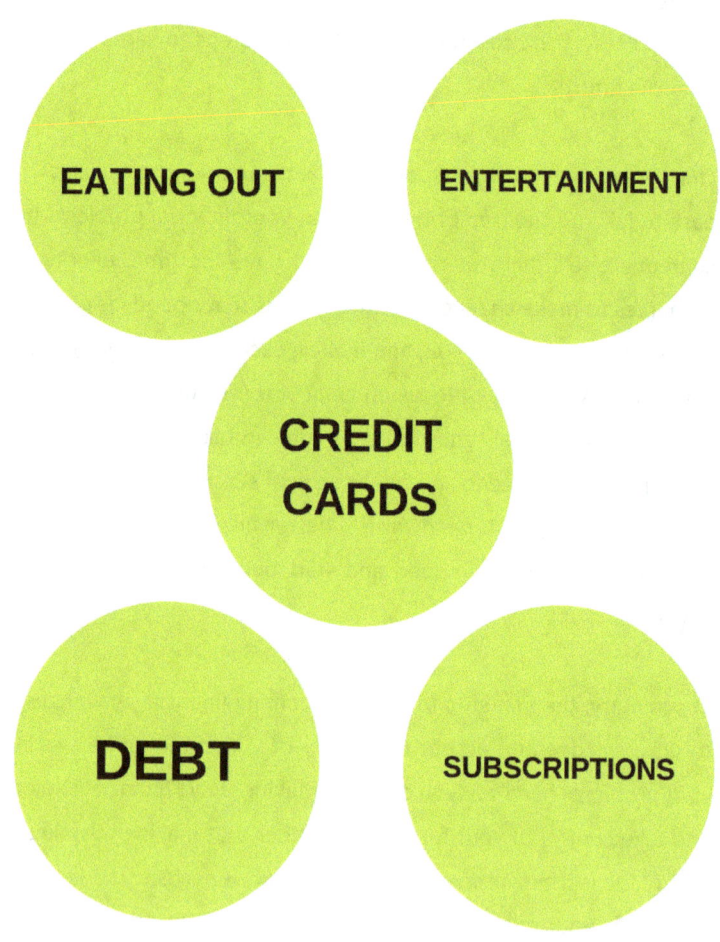

FACE YOUR REALITY: WHERE ARE YOU SPENDING?

Chapter 2
Exploring Your Options
& Making a Plan

Exploring Your Options: Listen, we understand that choosing a path and sticking to it is much more difficult than it sounds. We have been through countless situations where we had to make the choice to go one way or the other in ways that could drastically change our lives. Often, those choices had to be made quickly or the opportunities would vanish. Even more often, the choices involved our financial future, so there was tremendous pressure not to screw up the hard work that we've put into building our current progress in life.

Have we made choices that weren't the best? Absolutely. Have we learned from them and grown our decision-making muscles time after time? 100%. And we are confident that you will too!

Making tough choices is an inevitable part of managing your finances. It can be challenging to accept that you may have to make sacrifices in the short term to achieve long-term financial stability. However, it's essential to understand that making these choices doesn't define you as a person but rather helps you grow and learn.

Financial challenges can be overwhelming and stressful, but it's important to remember that you are not alone. Many people face financial difficulties at some point in their lives, and it's okay to ask for help or seek guidance. However, it's also important to take responsibility for your finances and take control of the situation.

Stopping and taking a deep breath can help clear your mind and approach the situation with a calm and focused mindset. Sometimes that deep breath can be taking a few hours to yourself, or you might need to step out of a difficult situation for a moment to reset. Accepting the situation doesn't mean giving up or ignoring the problem, but rather acknowledging that you are in a tough spot and need to take action. By accepting the situation, you can avoid the emotional and mental turmoil that can arise from denial or avoidance.

Making a Financial Plan

Imagine feeling like you're drowning in a sea of bills, expenses, and debt. Every day feels like a struggle to keep your head above water. You know you need to take control of your finances, but where do you even start? That's where having a plan comes in. It's like a life raft that can help you stay afloat and navigate your way towards financial stability.

A financial plan gives you direction and purpose. It helps you set goals and prioritize what's most important. And when you know what's important, it becomes easier to say "no" to unnecessary expenses and "yes" to the things that truly matter.

But a financial plan does more than just guide your spending. It also gives you peace of mind. When you have a plan, you can feel confident in your ability to handle unexpected expenses or emergencies. You won't have to worry about being caught off guard because you'll have a safety net in place.

And perhaps most importantly, a financial plan helps you make better decisions. No more impulsive purchases or emotional spending. With a plan in place, you can take a step back and evaluate the impact of your choices on your long-term financial goals.

So take a deep breath and make a plan. It may not be easy, but it's worth it. With a little determination and a solid financial plan, you can overcome any challenge and take control of your financial future.

Prioritize:

What is most important to you?

Exploring Your Options

One of the most important parts of creating a plan is exploring all of your options and understanding the pros and cons of each. For example, when facing debt, you may consider debt consolidation, bankruptcy, or refinancing, in addition to strategies for paying it off one at a time. Each option has its advantages and disadvantages, and it's crucial to weigh them carefully to make the best decision for your situation.

Once you have chosen a path forward, the next step is to create a plan and stick to it. This may involve prioritizing your debts, negotiating with creditors, cutting expenses, increasing income, and saving for emergencies. It's essential to set achievable goals and track your progress regularly.

Making tough financial choices can be difficult, but with the right mindset and a solid plan, you can overcome financial challenges and achieve long-term financial stability. Remember, every choice you make is an opportunity to learn and grow, and taking control of your finances is the first step towards a brighter future.

Let me tell you about friends of ours who were able to find financial success from making the right choices:

Jenna had always been careful with her finances, but when her husband lost his job, they found themselves drowning in debt. She felt overwhelmed and uncertain about what steps to take next. Should they consider debt consolidation, bankruptcy, or refinancing? She knew each option had its advantages and disadvantages, and it was crucial to weigh them carefully to make the best decision for their situation.

After doing her research and consulting with a financial advisor, Jenna and her husband decided to pursue debt consolidation. With a clear plan in place, Jenna felt a sense of relief and renewed motivation. She prioritized their debts, negotiated with creditors, and cut unnecessary expenses. She even picked up a part-time job to increase their income.

It wasn't easy, but with each payment they made, Jenna and her husband felt closer to achieving their goal of financial stability. They set achievable goals and tracked their progress regularly, celebrating each small victory along the way.

Eventually, they were able to pay off their debts and start saving for emergencies. Jenna felt empowered and grateful for the opportunity to learn and grow from this experience. She knew that making tough financial choices was never easy, but with the right mindset and a solid plan, they were able to overcome their financial challenges and build a brighter future for themselves and their family.

Tips for Success

- Identify your financial your values and aspirations.

- Find ways to reduce unnecessary spending.

- Set aside money for unexpected expenses.

- Explore ways to increase your income.

- Develop a plan to pay off debt.

- Start saving for short term goals.

- Monitor your financial plan as needed to stay on track towards your future goals.

WHAT ARE YOUR VALUES AND GOALS?

WHERE CAN YOU REDUCE YOUR SPENDING?

HOW CAN YOU INCREASE YOUR INCOME?

WHAT IS YOUR PLAN FOR PAYING OFF DEBT?

WHAT ARE YOUR VALUES AND PRIORITIES?

TRACK YOUR SAVINGS TOWARD YOUR GOALS:

Financial Advice

When it comes to seeking advice on financial matters, it's important to be careful who you listen to. While well-meaning friends and family members may offer their opinions, they may not necessarily be the most reliable sources of information. In fact, sometimes even so-called experts may not be trustworthy, and it's important to be able to distinguish between reliable and unreliable sources of guidance.

One of the best ways to evaluate the reliability of financial advice is to consider the credentials and track record of the source. For instance, a financial planner who is certified by a reputable organization, such as the Certified Financial Planner Board of Standards, is likely to have the education and experience necessary to offer sound advice. On the other hand, someone who claims to be a financial expert without any verifiable credentials or experience should be approached with caution.

If you're interested in learning more about the Certified Financial Planner (CFP) designation, you can visit the website of the Certified Financial Planner Board of Standards at https://www.cfp.net/. This website provides information on the requirements for earning and maintaining the CFP certification, as well as a directory of certified financial planners.

It's also important to consider the potential conflicts of interest that may be involved in financial advice. For example, a financial advisor who receives commissions for selling certain products or services may be biased in favor of those products, even if they are not the best option for you. In such cases, it may be wise to seek out a fee-only financial advisor, who charges a flat fee for their services and does not receive commissions or kickbacks.

Another factor to consider is the source's approach to risk. Some financial advisors may be more risk-averse than others and may advise you to take a more conservative approach to investing or debt management. While it's important to be prudent with your finances, it's also important to strike a balance between risk and reward, and to take calculated risks when appropriate. It's therefore important to find an advisor whose risk tolerance and goals align with your own.

Financial guidance could also come from sources other than a traditional investment advisor, like a mortgage lender, credit repair advisor, or a financially successful friend who has already achieved the stability you are looking for. When we are walking a client through making a home purchase in our real estate role, we will encourage the buyer to speak with a trusted mortgage lender who can talk them through what options they have for obtaining a mortgage. If the buyer is in need of a mortgage for their purchase, these lenders can be a very valuable source of information and guidance for the buyer. A lender can look over the buyer's income, assets, debts, and credit score and show the buyer which financing options are available to them. If the buyer is not able to qualify for a mortgage right away, the lender can explain what steps they would need to take to purchase a home in the future. This is a crucial first step of the home buying process and sets the direction for the entire home search.

Once a potential home buyer has their finances in order, they can meet with a Realtor® to make a plan for their home search. A good Realtor® will take the time to explain the home buying process to their client and listen to what the needs and goals are of their client. An attentive real estate agent can be an excellent source of advice when it comes to determining the best home purchasing decisions for their client. It's a good idea to interview a couple agents to choose someone you trust with walking you through this process.

The same goes for selling a house, which is just as significant a financial choice as buying. It can be even more so, as selling your property is the opportunity to make the best out of one of the biggest investments of your life. Again, you will want to choose a Realtor® who has your best interest in mind and can counsel you on the list price and marketing strategy will be best for you, your home, and the market you are in.

Of course, it's also important to trust your own instincts and do your own research. No one knows your financial situation and goals better than you do, and ultimately, it's up to you to make the decisions that are best for your circumstances. That being said, seeking advice from knowledgeable and trustworthy sources can help you make more informed decisions and avoid costly mistakes.

Adaptability to Change

In addition to seeking out reliable sources of guidance, it's also important to be flexible and adaptable to changing circumstances. Life is unpredictable, and financial situations can change rapidly. It's therefore important to regularly review and adjust your financial plan as needed.

For example, let's say you've made a plan to pay off your credit card debt within a certain timeframe. However, if unexpected expenses or a job loss occur, you may need to adjust your plan to avoid falling further into debt. By regularly reviewing your finances and adjusting your plan as needed, you can stay on track and make progress toward your goals, even in the face of unexpected challenges.

Seeking reliable financial advice and being adaptable to changing circumstances are key to achieving financial success. By carefully evaluating sources of guidance and regularly reviewing and adjusting your financial plan, you can make informed decisions and stay on track toward your goals. Remember, ultimately, it's up to you to take control of your finances and make the choices that are best for your situation.

Introducing The Choice Map

Are you facing a difficult financial decision and feeling overwhelmed by the choices ahead? We have created the Choice Map to be a guide for you when you are evaluating which life choice is best for any given situation, but particularly with your finances.

The Choice Map is a powerful tool that can help you navigate difficult financial decisions with clarity and confidence. Once you have identified your goal and evaluated your options, the Choice Map helps you to create a plan of action and stay on track. Celebrating your achievements along the way and learning from your experiences will enable you to improve your decision-making skills and face future challenges with confidence.

We are excited to present The Choice Map to you to help you take control of your finances and build a brighter financial future. We will dive into each of the six steps in the next chapter!

Building a strong financial foundation starts with setting goals, creating a budget, automating your savings, and being mindful of your spending.

Chapter 3
The Choice Map

Welcome to the third chapter of our journey toward financial recovery and success! This section is arguably the most crucial part of the book, as it introduces the powerful tool known as the Choice Map. By using the Choice Map, you will be able to navigate the complexities of financial decision-making with confidence and clarity.

Why is this section the most important, you ask? Well, the Choice Map provides a step-by-step framework that will help you make well-informed and intentional choices based on your values, goals, and circumstances. It will also equip you with the skills necessary to evaluate the short- and long-term consequences of your decisions, anticipate future challenges, and learn from your experiences. The Choice Map is a versatile tool that can be applied to any financial decision you may face, whether it's related to buying a car, saving for retirement, investing in stocks, or paying off debt, to name a few. It is also adaptable to different stages of your financial journey, from starting out to scaling up to maintaining success.

In this chapter, you will learn how to acknowledge the reality of your situation, know your options and strategies, understand the challenges and obstacles, make a plan and follow it, celebrate your achievements, and anticipate the next choice. By following these steps, you will be able to achieve the ultimate goal of this book: financial freedom and peace of mind.

So, are you ready to embark on this exciting and transformative journey? Let's dive into the Choice Map and discover the power of intentional choice-making!

THE C.H.O.I.C.E. MAP

C   CLARIFY your goals & priorities
H   HONE IN on your options & alternatives
O   OBSERVE the challenges & obstacles
I   IDENTIFY a plan & take action
C   CELEBRATE your achievement & accept your choice
E   EVALUATE the outcome & learn from experience

Step 1: CLARIFY Your Goals & Priorities

Why are you making this choice? What matters most to you?

The first step in any decision-making process is to acknowledge why you're making the choice that is in front of you, and what part of the situation matters most to you. This helps you to determine the heart behind the decision so you have a groundwork upon which to base your decision. This step requires self-reflection and introspection, which can be difficult but ultimately rewarding. Without a clear understanding of your motivation and values, it's challenging to make a decision that aligns with your goals and aspirations.

It's essential to acknowledge and accept the reality of your situation. Many people struggle with denial or avoidance when it comes to their financial situation. They may not want to face the fact that they're in debt or living paycheck to paycheck. However, avoiding the problem won't make it go away, and it can even make things worse. Acknowledging your situation is the first step toward taking control and making a positive change.

To get started with this step, take some time to reflect on your values and priorities. What's most important to you? Is it financial security, freedom, success, happiness, family, or something else? Think about why you want to make this decision and what you hope to achieve.

For example, suppose you're considering a career change. In that case, you need to acknowledge why you're considering this change and what matters most to you. Perhaps you're unhappy in your current job and you value work that makes a difference in the world. Or maybe you're looking for more work-life balance and flexibility so you can spend more time with your family. When you can verbalize what you're looking to get out of the decision, then you can also identify what you are willing to give up to achieve that outcome. In the previous example, if you're looking for more self-fulfillment or time flexibility, maybe you are willing to accept lower pay or less benefits. Only you and anyone making the decision with you, like a spouse or partner, can determine what is most important to you.

Let's say you're considering buying a new car. The first step is to acknowledge and explore why you're making this choice and what matters most to you. You might realize that having reliable transportation is important to you because you need to commute to work or take your kids to school. You might also value safety and comfort, as well as your image and social status. However, you also need to acknowledge the reality of your situation, which includes your budget, your credit score, your existing debts, and your long-term financial goals. You might discover that buying a new car is not the most practical or affordable option for you now. You might have to consider alternative solutions, such as buying a used car, leasing a car, or improving your credit score and saving up for a down payment.

By acknowledging the reality of your situation, you avoid denial or avoidance, which can make things worse. For example, if you ignore your budget and credit score and impulsively buy a new car, you might end up with a high-interest loan, monthly payments that strain your budget, and a depreciating asset that loses value over time. You might also experience regret, stress, and conflicts with your family and friends.

On the other hand, if you take the time to focus on the situation through the lens of how the outcome can align with your values and goals, you can make an informed and empowered decision. You can explore your options and strategies based on your financial situation and priorities. You can also seek professional help if needed, such as a financial planner, a counselor, a lawyer, or a car dealer who respects your choices and preferences.

By taking the time to acknowledge and explore your motivations and constraints, you can gain clarity and confidence in your decision-making process. You can also learn from your experience and improve your financial literacy and self-awareness. Ultimately, by making a well-informed and intentional choice, you can achieve your goal of financial recovery and well-being.

In summary, Step 1 of the Choice Map is all about acknowledging why you're making a choice and what matters most to you before you move forward with any decisions. This step helps you align your choices with your values and goals, giving you a solid foundation for making the best possible decision for your unique circumstances. By acknowledging and accepting the reality of your situation, you can take the first step toward your goals and aspirations.

THE C.H.O.I.C.E. MAP

CLARIFY
YOUR GOALS & PRIORITIES

_____
_____
_____
_____
_____
_____
_____
_____
_____

Step 2: HONE IN on Your Options & Alternatives

Having a clear and realistic goal for your financial recovery is important to help you identify the options and strategies that you can take to achieve it. Once you know what you want to accomplish, you can begin to research and evaluate the different options available to you.

Let's go back to the example we discussed earlier of deciding whether you should purchase a car. You might start by researching the different financing options available, such as leasing, financing, or saving up to buy the car outright. Then, weigh the pros and cons of each option.

I'm going to break down the various options like I would if I was evaluating this decision with you:

Leasing
This option allows you to drive a new car for a fixed period (usually 2-3 years) and pay only for the depreciation and fees, rather than the full cost of the car.

Pros: Lower monthly payments, less money upfront, option to upgrade to a new car at the end of the lease.

Cons: No ownership equity, mileage limits, extra fees for excessive wear and tear, no customization options.

Financing

This option involves borrowing money from a lender (such as a bank, credit union, or dealership) to buy the car and paying back the loan with interest over time.

Pros: Ownership equity, flexible terms, potential for better interest rates with good credit, opportunity to improve credit score with timely payments.

Cons: Higher monthly payments, more money upfront, risk of negative equity, default and repossession, interest charges can add up over time.

Saving for Cash Purchase

This option involves setting aside money over time until you can afford to buy the car outright, without borrowing or leasing.

Pros: No debt or monthly payments, no interest charges, more flexibility in choosing the car and negotiating the price, potential for earning interest on savings.

Cons: Longer time to achieve the goal, opportunity cost of not investing or using the money for other purposes, risk of losing value due to inflation or market changes.

Buying Used

This option involves buying a pre-owned car from a private party or dealership, instead of a brand new car. This option can also be combined with one of the options above.

Pros: Lower price, potential for better value for the money, less depreciation, more room for negotiation, more options in terms of models and features.

Cons: Higher risk of mechanical issues or hidden problems, less warranty coverage, potential for higher maintenance and repair costs, less customization options.

Sharing

This option involves using alternative modes of transportation, such as carpooling, ridesharing, public transit, biking, or walking, instead of owning a car.

Pros: Lower cost, more environmentally friendly, potential for social connections and reduced traffic congestion, no maintenance or insurance cost.

Cons: Less convenience, less privacy, limited range, potential for delays or disruptions.

Once you have identified your options, you need to evaluate their short-term and long-term consequences. For example, if you choose to lease a car, you need to consider the total cost of the lease over time, including the monthly payments, fees, and potential penalties for early termination or excess mileage. On the other hand, if you choose to save up for a new car, you need to consider the potential for inflation and changes in market conditions, as well as the potential for losing the opportunity to invest or being able to use the money for other purposes. In general, you should choose the option that aligns with your values and goals, and that provides the best balance between short-term benefits and long-term outcomes.

Additionally, you should consider how each option fits into your overall financial goals and values. For example, if you value financial stability and independence, you may want to prioritize paying off your debts and saving for emergencies before committing to a new car payment. If you value convenience and comfort, you may be willing to make some sacrifices in other areas to afford a nicer car.

In summary, knowing your options and the strategies available to you is crucial in making a sound financial decision. Taking the time to research and evaluate each option based on its pros and cons, short- and long-term consequences, and how it fits into your overall financial goals and values, will help you make the best decision for your situation.

THE C.H.O.I.C.E. MAP

HONE IN
ON YOUR OPTIONS & ALTERNATIVES

_____
_____
_____
_____
_____
_____
_____
_____
_____
_____

Step 3: OBSERVE the Challenges & Obstacles

Understanding the challenges and obstacles is an essential step in making any decision. It helps you anticipate the difficulties you might face and plan accordingly. However, it is also important to remember that no matter how well you plan, unexpected problems may arise. The key is to have a positive attitude and be open to finding solutions. In this step, we will explore how to identify and overcome common obstacles that can prevent you from achieving your goals.

Fear of Failure: This fear can be paralyzing and prevent you from taking action toward your goals. It is important to recognize that failure is a natural part of the learning process and that every mistake is an opportunity to learn and grow. Instead of letting fear hold you back, use it as motivation to work harder and smarter toward your goals.

Lack of Resources: Another challenge that people face is the lack of resources, whether it be time, money, or support. It can be discouraging when you feel like you don't have the necessary resources to achieve your goals. However, it is important to remember that resourcefulness is a valuable skill, and there are always ways to work around limitations. For example, if you don't have the money to invest in a project, you can try to find creative ways to raise funds or collaborate with others who share your vision.

Lack of Knowledge or Capability: Additionally, a lack of knowledge or skills can also be a significant obstacle. It can be overwhelming when you feel like you don't know where to start or how to move forward. However, there are many resources available, such as books, courses, and mentors that can help you acquire the knowledge and skills you need. It is essential to be willing to learn and be open to feedback and constructive criticism.

Affordability: This is one of the most common challenges that people face when making any financial decision. Whether it's buying a house, starting a business, or going back to school, the cost can be daunting. To overcome this challenge, it's important to create a realistic budget and explore different financing options, such as loans, grants, scholarships, or crowdfunding. You may also want to consider downsizing, cutting back on unnecessary expenses, or taking on a side job to increase your income.

Uncertainty: Another challenge that people often face is the fear of the unknown. They may feel uncertain about the outcome of their decision or worry that they will regret it later. To overcome this challenge, it's important to do your research and gather as much information as possible about your options. You may also want to seek advice from trusted friends, family members, or professionals, such as financial advisors or career counselors.

Procrastination: This is a common obstacle that can prevent people from making any decision at all. They may feel overwhelmed by the choices or uncertain about their ability to follow through. To overcome this obstacle, it's important to break the decision down into smaller, manageable steps, and set specific deadlines for each one. You may also want to enlist the help of an accountability partner, such as a friend or mentor, who can support you and hold you accountable.

Self-Limitations: Lastly, negative self-talk and limiting beliefs can also hinder your progress toward your goals. It is crucial to be aware of your thoughts and how they can influence your emotions and actions. Instead of letting negative self-talk hold you back, try to reframe your thoughts in a positive way. Focus on your strengths and accomplishments and use positive affirmations to help you stay motivated and confident.

In summary, understanding the challenges and obstacles you may face is an essential step in achieving your goals. By recognizing common obstacles and learning how to overcome them, you can develop the resilience and resourcefulness needed to succeed. Remember to stay positive, be open to learning and feedback, and stay focused on your goals.

THE C.H.O.I.C.E. MAP

OBSERVE
THE CHALLENGES & OBSTACLES

_____
_____
_____
_____
_____
_____
_____
_____
_____

Step 4: IDENTIFY a Plan & Take Action

Step 4 of the Choice Map is where you take the knowledge and understanding you have gained from Steps 1-3 and use it to create a plan of action. This is a crucial step in achieving your goal, as without a clear plan of what you need to do, it can be easy to get sidetracked or lose motivation.

Creating a plan of action may seem daunting, but it can be broken down into several smaller steps. First, you need to identify your goal and what you want to achieve. This could be anything from starting your own business to paying off debt or saving for a down payment on a house. Whatever your goal is, it should be specific, measurable, and achievable.

Once you have identified your goal, you need to create a roadmap for achieving it. This involves breaking down your goal into smaller, more manageable steps, and setting deadlines for each one. For example, if your goal is to start your own business, and you've already made the decision from the first 3 Steps that this is the right decision for you, then your roadmap might include researching your market, creating a business plan, securing funding, and launching your product or service.

Step 4
MAKE A PLAN OF ACTION

30 DAYS
ACTION PLAN
-
-
-
-

60 DAYS
ACTION PLAN
-
-
-
-

90 DAYS
ACTION PLAN
-
-
-
-

It is important to be flexible and adaptable when creating your plan of action, as unexpected obstacles or changes in circumstances can occur. You may need to adjust your plan along the way, but by having a clear roadmap, you can stay focused and motivated, and continue moving toward your goal.

Another important aspect of creating a plan of action is to be held accountable. This means setting up systems and processes to track your progress and holding yourself responsible for achieving your milestones. This could involve creating a daily or weekly to-do list, using a project management tool, or working with a coach or accountability partner.

In summary, Step 4 of the Choice Map is all about creating a plan of action to achieve your goal. By breaking down your goal into smaller steps, setting deadlines, being flexible, and holding yourself accountable, you can stay focused and motivated, and make steady progress toward achieving your goal.

Let's continue with the example of starting your own business. Here is what it could look like to outline steps for yourself to create a plan of action:

Identify your goals: What do you want to achieve with your business? Do you want to make a certain amount of money, provide a specific product or service, or create a work-life balance?

Understanding your goals will help you create a plan that is tailored to your needs.

Research the market: Before starting a business, it's important to research the market to determine if there is a demand for your product or service. You can do this by conducting surveys, analyzing industry reports, and monitoring competitor activity.

Create a budget: Starting a business requires financial investment. You need to create a budget that outlines your start-up costs, such as office space, equipment, inventory, and marketing expenses. You also need to consider your ongoing expenses, such as salaries, rent, and utilities.

Develop a business plan: A business plan outlines your goals, strategies, and financial projections. It's important to create a comprehensive plan that includes details such as your target market, marketing strategy, operations plan, and financial projections.

Secure funding: Once you have a budget and business plan in place, you need to secure funding to start your business. You can do this by applying for a business loan, seeking investment from venture capitalists, or using your own personal savings.

Choose a location: Will you need a brick-and-mortar storefront, or will you be working from home? If you need a physical place of business, you will need to identify what type of building and location are best suited to your business's success. However, if you are able to work remotely, you will need to establish where you will be able to focus on your work and be productive, as well as store inventory if you are selling a product.

Launch your business: After you have secured funding, it's time to launch your business. This includes setting up your website, launching your marketing campaign, and opening your doors to customers – whether physically or virtually.

Monitor your progress: Once your business is up and running, it's important to monitor your progress to ensure you are achieving your goals. This includes tracking your financials, monitoring customer feedback, and analyzing your marketing efforts.

By following these steps and creating a plan of action, you can increase your chances of success when starting your own business.

THE C.H.O.I.C.E. MAP

IDENTIFY
A PLAN & TAKE ACTION

_____
_____
_____
_____
_____
_____
_____
_____
_____
_____

Step 5: CELEBRATE Your Achievement & Accept Your Choice

When making a significant life choice, it's easy to get bogged down by the details and forget to celebrate the progress you've made. Taking a step back and acknowledging how far you've come can help you stay motivated and build momentum in your life.

Step 5 of the Choice Map is crucial for your long-term financial success because it involves accepting and celebrating the outcome of your decision-making process. By this point, you have already gone through the previous steps of acknowledging why you are making the choice, knowing your options and strategies, understanding the challenges and obstacles, and making a plan of action. Now, it's time to celebrate your achievements and accept the results.

Celebration

Celebrating your achievement is of vital importance because it reinforces the positive aspects of your decision and motivates you to continue making progress toward your financial goals. Celebration doesn't have to be grandiose or expensive. It can be as simple as taking a moment to appreciate the benefits of your choice, such as the peace of mind that comes with being debt-free, the joy of owning a home, or the sense of accomplishment from achieving a long-term goal.

Let's say you've decided to save money for a down payment on a house. After going through the Choice Map, you've acknowledged that owning a home is important to you because it provides stability and security for your family. You've researched your options and strategies, such as saving a percentage of your income each month and reducing your expenses. You've also anticipated and prepared for challenges, such as unexpected expenses or fluctuations in the housing market. Finally, you've created a plan of action that includes setting a savings goal, tracking your progress, and adjusting your budget as needed.

Now that you've saved enough money and bought your dream home, it's time to celebrate your achievement and accept your choice. You can celebrate by having a housewarming party with your friends and family, decorating your new home, or taking a break and enjoying some quality time with your loved ones. You can also accept your choice by acknowledging the challenges and sacrifices you made along the way and being grateful for the rewards that come with homeownership.

Acceptance
Accepting your choice can be challenging, especially if it didn't go as planned or if you have any regrets or doubts. However, it's essential to acknowledge that you did the best you could with the information and resources available to you at the time. By accepting the choice you've made, you can move forward with a clear mind and a positive attitude, which can help you make better decisions in the future.

It is understandable if this is difficult, especially if your choice didn't turn out the way you had hoped. However, dwelling on regrets or second-guessing yourself will only hold you back from moving forward. You can also acknowledge what you did right or wrong so you have the opportunity to start back at Step 1 in the future with eyes wide open the next time you enter into a similar situation.

To accept your choice, try to focus on the positive aspects of your decision and what you've learned from the experience. You can also practice self-compassion, acknowledging that everyone makes mistakes and that it's okay to not have all the answers. Finally, try to reframe any negative thoughts or emotions as opportunities for growth and learning.

For example, let's say you're trying to get in shape and lose weight. Celebrating your progress could mean acknowledging the healthy habits you've built, such as going for a daily walk or eating more vegetables. It could also mean tracking your progress with photos, measurements, or a fitness app, and celebrating milestones along the way, such as hitting a new personal best or fitting into a different size of clothing. However, as we well know and have experienced, there are times when we don't stick to our goals as closely as we would like and make poor choices about diet or exercise. It's so easy to get ourselves down about this, but if we become stuck in the disappointment of failures, we will often find ourselves right back where we began. Instead, it's crucial to keep a positive attitude and choose wisely in the future. This is how goals are achieved and overall trends continue in the direction we are aiming for.

In summary, Step 5 of the Choice Map is about accepting and celebrating your decision, whether it's buying a new car, starting a business, or saving for a down payment on a house. By doing so, you can boost your confidence, reinforce positive behavior, and move forward with a clear mind and a positive attitude.

THE C.H.O.I.C.E. MAP

CELEBRATE

YOUR ACHIEVEMENT &
ACCEPT YOUR CHOICE

Step 6: EVALUATE the Outcome & Learn from Your Experience

The final step of the Choice Map is all about anticipating your next choice and learning from your experience. After making a decision and taking action, it is important to reflect on the process and outcomes in order to improve your future choices. By doing so, you can become more mindful of your decision-making process and increase your chances of success in the future.

To anticipate your next choice, it is important to understand the potential outcomes of your current decision and how it may affect your future options. For example, if you have decided to pursue a new career path, it is important to anticipate the challenges and opportunities that may arise from this decision, such as a different demand on your time, acquiring new skills, networking, or starting a new business.

In addition, it is important to plan for the future and consider how you can be better prepared for the next choice. This may involve researching new strategies, tools, or resources that can help you achieve your goals more effectively. For instance, if you are planning to invest in a new business, you may need to anticipate the potential risks and benefits of this decision and develop a contingency plan to mitigate any potential losses.

To learn from your experience, it is important to reflect on your decision-making process and the outcomes of your actions. You can ask yourself questions such as:

What worked well?
What could have been done differently?
What lessons did I learn?
What would I do differently next time?

Feel free to use the worksheet on the next page as a guideline.

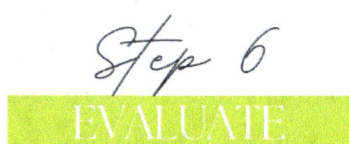
Step 6
EVALUATE

1 What worked well?
....
....
....

2 What could have been done differently?
....
....
....

3 What lessons did I learn?
....
....
....

4 What would I do differently next time?
....
....
....

In addition, seeking feedback from others can also be helpful in improving your decision-making skills. This can include talking to a mentor, a coach, or a trusted friend or family member. By gathering different perspectives and insights, you can gain a better understanding of your strengths and weaknesses, and develop a more informed approach to decision-making.

In summary, Step 6 of the Choice Map emphasizes the importance of anticipating the next choice and learning from your experience. By doing so, you can become more mindful of your decision-making process, and develop more effective strategies for achieving your goals.

THE C.H.O.I.C.E. MAP

EVALUATE
THE OUTCOME & LEARN FROM EXPERIENCE

THE C.H.O.I.C.E MAP

Step 1: CLARIFY Your Goals & Priorities
Why are you making this choice? What matters most to you? This step involves reflecting on your values and priorities, and being honest with yourself about why you are making a particular financial decision.

Step 2: HONE IN on Your Options & Alternatives
This step involves gathering information and evaluating the available options and strategies for achieving your financial goals.

Step 3: OBSERVE the Challenges & Obstacles
This step involves anticipating and preparing for the potential difficulties and setbacks that may arise during the decision-making process.

Step 4: IDENTIFY a Plan & Take Action
This step involves creating a clear and actionable plan of action based on the information and insights gathered in the previous steps.

Step 5: CELEBRATE Your Achievement & Accept Your Choice
Celebrate your achievement and acceptance of your choice. This step involves acknowledging and appreciating the progress and successes achieved so far, and accepting the choice made with confidence and self-assurance.

Step 6: EVALUATE the Outcome & Learn From Your Experience

Evaluate the outcome of the decision you made, anticipate the next choice and learn from your experience. This step involves looking ahead to the next financial decision you may face and applying the lessons learned from this process to make more informed and effective decisions in the future.

Now that you have learned about the 6 Steps of the Choice Map, we'd like to outline how this looks in real life with your own Tough Financial Choices.

Example 1: Choosing a College Major

Using the CHOICE acronym, here is how a thoughtful and informed decision process can look like when choosing a college major:

Step 1: CLARIFY your goals and priorities
Narrow down your choices to a few majors that align with your values, interests, and career goals. In this case, the options are Psychology, Business, and Communications.

Step 2: HONE IN your options and alternatives
Ask yourself questions like what the potential career paths and opportunities are for each major. Find professionals in each field and discuss with them what education and experience are necessary to be successful in their field. Be open to alternatives you have not previously considered, like if a college degree might not be necessary and experience is more important.

Step 3: OBSERVE the challenges & obstacles
Outline what the potential challenges and risks are of each major, such as competition, salary, or job satisfaction. Are there obstacles in the way of reaching success? Perhaps the length of schooling or amount of financial investment are not what you are capable or willing to take on.

Step 4: IDENTIFY a plan & take action

Based on your answers, create a plan that includes researching job descriptions, salaries, and career growth projections for each major, networking with professionals in each field, participating in internships or extracurricular activities, and attending career fairs and workshops to learn about current trends and demands. Once you've identified the career path you would like to pursue, make your college major selection and get started with classes!

Step 5: CELEBRATE your achievement & accept your choice

Celebrate that you've made such a life-changing decision and taken the step of starting classes toward a career you are excited about! Accept the results of that choice, including the class workload, cost of schooling, competitive job market, and pressures of the career you've chosen.

Step 6: EVALUATE the outcome and learn from your experience

After making your decision, reflect on your decision-making process and evaluate the outcomes. For example, if you chose Psychology and find it difficult to find a job after graduation, reflect on what factors contributed to this outcome. Start the Choice Map again to determine whether to continue in that field or if a pivot needs to be made. Anticipate the next choice and learn from your experience. This step involves looking ahead to the next financial decision you may face and applying the lessons learned from this process to make more informed and effective decisions in the future.

Example 2: Buying a Home

Step 1: CLARIFY your goals and priorities
Before making a decision to purchase a home, clarify your decision-making criteria and goals. We recommend meeting with a local Realtor® to discuss your potential home search and learn about the home buying process. A good real estate agent will ask you why you want to buy a home, what in your life makes this the right time for you, and what you are looking for in your next home. These questions are important to evaluate so you can enter into the home buying process with eyes on your goals.

Step 2: HONE IN your options and alternatives
After clarifying your criteria and goals, hone in on your options and alternatives. If you have already determined that your goal is to be able to purchase a house with a certain amount of money out of pocket and within your monthly budget, then stick to that and look within the price range that boundary provides. There is no purpose to looking at beautiful pictures of homes outside the budget that your previously established goals have determined.

Within that budget, now research different types of homes, such as single-family houses, condos, or townhouses. You might also look into different neighborhoods or areas to find the best fit for your needs and preferences. You can also consider your lifestyle and future plans, such as the need for extra space or the possibility of expanding your family.

Step 3: OBSERVE the challenges & obstacles

After gathering information and options, organize the information and weigh the pros and cons of each alternative. Consider factors like price, location, size, condition, and community amenities. You might also compare the benefits and drawbacks of each type of home, such as maintenance costs, property taxes, or HOA fees. No home is perfect, so prioritize what is most important to you and recognize what you're open to compromising on.

Step 4: IDENTIFY a plan & take action

Once you find a home within your budget that is a good fit for your needs and goals, then it's time to sit down with your Realtor® and make an offer! They can walk you through even more Choices as you determine with them what the right offer is to make. Remember to keep your goals and priorities in mind!

Step 5: CELEBRATE your achievement & accept your choice

Once your offer is accepted and you've processed the necessary paperwork, you can close on your new home and it is yours! This is a great time to celebrate! Host a house-warming party, or at least celebrate with pizza on the floor of your new living room with your friends who helped you move. Of course, as you get settled in, you're bound to find imperfections in the home or be faced with the reality that there are inconveniences here and there. Remember that you weighed the home-buying decisions carefully with your real estate agent and that you made the best purchase you could at the time.

Step 6: EVALUATE the outcome and learn from your experience

By learning from your experience, you can reflect on your decision-making process and evaluate the outcomes of your choice. For example, if you choose a townhouse and later realize that the community rules are too restrictive, you can reflect on what factors contributed to this outcome, such as your expectations or the management style. You can use this information to make a more informed and strategic choice in the future. Or perhaps you love your home and are proud of the decision you made. Great! Use this success as a reminder to implement the Choice Map in more decisions you have to make in the future.

Throughout this chapter, we have explored the six steps of the Choice Map, which is a practical framework for making effective and satisfying decisions in any area of life, including personal finance. By following these six steps, you can make well-informed and satisfying financial decisions that align with your values and priorities, and set yourself up for success in the long run. Remember, making good financial choices is a journey, not a destination, and every step counts towards a brighter financial future.

The key point to remember with the Choice Map is that it is a tool to be used over and over again. Working through the Map once and being choice-free for the rest of your life is not how it works. You need to be constantly evaluating the options in your life and taking the necessary steps to make tough financial choices. The more you work through these steps, the more it will become a natural process for your decision making.

If you find that the outcome of your choices are consistently negative, then it is crucial that you evaluate very closely where in the Map you are taking the wrong turn. Are you failing to learn from your past experiences and making the same poor choice over and over? Are you not taking the time to look deeply into each of the obstacles and challenges that might arise under each option, glossing over the potential negatives so you can choose the easier or more attractive option? These mistakes can be detrimental if you refuse to acknowledge them and work intentionally to avoid them in the future.

"Life is a series of choices, and every financial decision you make either leads you closer to your goals or further away from them."

Chapter 4
Running Out of Room

So, you've made some poor financial decisions in the past, and now you're feeling stuck. It happens to the best of us. Maybe you took out a loan you couldn't afford, made a risky investment, or simply spent finances beyond your means. Whatever it was, the important thing is that you're ready to move forward and make better choices. Here are some tips to help you get back on track:

Firstly, don't beat yourself up about it. We all make mistakes, and dwelling on them will only hold you back. Instead, focus on the lessons you learned from your mistakes. What could you have done differently? How can you avoid making the same mistake in the future? Use your experience to become a smarter and more informed financial decision-maker.

Next, create a budget. This may not sound like the most exciting thing in the world, but trust us, it's essential. A budget will help you track your expenses, identify areas where you can cut back, and stay on top of your bills. Plus, it doesn't have to be all spreadsheets and numbers - get creative with it! Maybe you use colorful markers to track your spending or make a game out of saving money. Find what works for you.

Another way to move forward is to seek support. This could be in the form of a financial advisor, a support group, or simply a trusted friend or family member who can provide guidance and encouragement. Having someone in your corner can make all the difference.

Finally, don't forget to celebrate your successes along the way. It's easy to get bogged down in the negatives and forget to recognize the positives. Did you pay off a debt? Treat yourself to a small indulgence. Meet a savings goal?

Take yourself out for a fancy dinner. Celebrating your progress will keep you motivated and remind you of how far you've come. Remember, just because you've made poor financial decisions in the past doesn't mean you're doomed to a lifetime of financial struggle. By taking steps to learn from your mistakes, create a budget, seek support, and celebrate your successes, you can move forward with confidence and make better choices for your financial future.

I want you to know that I understand the struggles and challenges you may be facing right now. I know what it's like to feel stuck, hopeless, and unsure of how to move forward. That's why we wrote this book - to offer guidance and support to anyone who may be feeling lost or overwhelmed in their financial journey.

1. EMBRACE BUDGETING
2. BE MINDFUL OF YOUR SPENDING
3. STAY ACCOUNTABLE
4. ADJUST YOUR LIFESTYLE
5. SET REALISTIC GOALS
6. CELEBRATE YOUR PROGRESS.

Remember the stories of the couples in the Introduction that were struggling financially? As it turns out, both of these stories were actually about us. We were the newly married couple struggling to make ends meet and the couple making poor choices to live up to the American dream. We know firsthand how difficult it can be to feel trapped in a situation and unsure of how to move forward.

But we also learned that the choices we make today have a profound impact on our future. This is WHY we created the Choice Map, because that is the process that we had to create for ourselves to get out of each season of financial struggle. Remember that - the position you are in right now is a season of your life, not where you are stuck for the rest of your future.

Once we set the goal to become financially stable and get ourselves out of the burden of debt, we knew we had to make many small choices that would eventually turn the direction of our lives around. By choosing over and over to make sacrifices, cut expenses, live modestly, and focus on our long-term goals as the reward, we were able to pull ourselves out of debt and start building a life that we could be proud of. It certainly wasn't easy and there were absolutely times when we felt like giving up, but we persisted, knowing that every choice we made brought us one step closer to our dreams. And we can tell you from experience that it's worth it.

Remember when we said we sketched a drawing of our dream home back when we were first married and struggling to make ends meet?

Well, we found that drawing in a box recently after moving and held it up. Tears came to our eyes as we looked at each other and realized that we were standing in that same home. Dreams like that don't just come true with the passing of time. Dreams become a reality by digging deep, recognizing your mistakes, and doing the hard work to get where you have always longed to be in the freedom of financial security.

So, if you're feeling stuck or uncertain about your future, know that you're not alone. We've been there, and we know how hard it can be. But we also what you to know that there is a light at the end of the tunnel, and that the choices you make today can help you get there.

Remember that every small choice you make can add up to big results over time. So, take a step back, evaluate your priorities, and start making choices that will help you achieve your goals. Yes, you will most likely have to make sacrifices in the short term, but in the long run, you'll be so glad you did.

Just like our story, you may feel like you're stuck in a difficult situation. You've made some choices that maybe weren't the best, but you did the best with the knowledge you had at the time. And now, you're faced with the consequences of those choices.

But here's the thing: it's not too late to turn things around. You can make tough choices now that will help you focus on the deep, fulfilling satisfaction of goals and dreams reached, instead of just satisfying immediate wants and needs. It won't be easy, and it requires sacrifice, but it will be worth it in the end.

Think about your goals and what you want for your family. Maybe it's a stable home where your kids can grow up without hearing you worry about finances. Maybe it's being able to provide for them without the burden of credit card companies calling to collect or having to ask for yet another loan extension. Whatever it is, keep that vision in mind as you make decisions going forward.

"Small actions can lead to big financial gains. Invest in yourself and your future, one dollar at a time."

Chapter 5
Make The Choice

Congratulations! You have taken the necessary steps to improve your financial situation, and that is an accomplishment in and of itself. It takes courage and determination to make tough financial choices and overcome challenges, and you have done just that. Acknowledging and appreciating your progress can boost your confidence and self-esteem, which in turn can help you stay motivated and focused on your financial goals.

As we come to the end of this book, it's important to reflect on the valuable lessons and insights that we've gained about financial recovery. We've learned about the importance of facing our financial challenges head-on, taking responsibility for our actions, and making tough choices to improve our financial well-being.

We started out by facing the reality of our financial situations, reflecting on where we were at the beginning of this journey. We started out by being honest with ourselves about our current situation and what got us there, being open with others about our situation, and being ready to embrace the change as we moved forward. We then reviewed common financial problems and how they impact our lives. Maybe you resonated with one of those or it sparked understanding of how your circumstances have affected your financial status.

Next, we looked at the 3 Types of Financial Choices: Forced, Poor, & Smart. It's important to take a step back before making a tough financial choice to evaluate if we absolutely must make the choice or if it's optional, and then do our best to make a smart decision instead of a poor choice that leaves us stuck with the consequences.

In Chapter 2, we launched into how to review all our options before making a financial plan that can benefit our lives long-term and reach our overall goals. That came with a warning, however, to be cautious of who you take advice from. Not all who want to guide you in your finances are reputable sources that you should be listening to, so evaluate carefully before you allow them to direct you one way or another. Ultimately, when planning out your finances, it is important to be flexible to change and pivot as needed for you to continually grow.

Launching into the Choice Map, our heart was to provide you with a tool that you can reference time and time again as you work through your options to make wise financial decisions. The best way to become skilled at making good decisions is to start with one small decision, and then just keep working through the 6 Steps on each choice that comes your way as you become comfortable with the steps and it becomes second nature. We hope you found the Choice Map to be a helpful guideline to empower you to make smart decisions throughout your life and grow your financial future.

The Choice Map
C - CLARIFY your goals and priorities
H - HONE IN on your options and alternatives
O - OBSERVE the challenges & obstacles
I - IDENTIFY a plan & take action
C - CELEBRATE your achievement & accept your choice
E - EVALUATE the outcome & learn from your experience

We also discussed how we understand that you might be feeling stuck right now in your current situation, like life dealt you horrible circumstances or that you've already made too many poor choices. It might feel like there is no way out and you'll never achieve the dreams that you once had. Our heart is that you start to see that there is always a way out. You can improve your circumstances by patiently walking through the steps in this book. It might not turn things around overnight, but life is a series of small choices building upon one another.

Remember, we've been there. We've been stuck at the very beginning with no direction of how we could even begin to build a future living on the smallest resources. We've also been drowning in debt, in over our heads with expenses from buying too big, living well beyond our means. We realized something major had to change so we could provide the life we have always wanted for our family within financial stability. Taking the time and serious effort to work through the Choice Map ourselves and make the changes necessary, we have been able to experience the life-changing benefits of being financially free. We share this because we know that you can do this too! We want this so much for you. You do not need to be a slave to your past decisions or unavoidable circumstances. You CAN be in control of creating the future you have always dreamed of by making the right choices going forward.

So, take a moment to reflect on your journey so far, and celebrate the progress and achievements you have made. You've got this!

Remember, financial recovery is not a destination, but an ongoing journey. It requires continuous effort and a commitment to making positive changes in our financial habits and mindset. With the right tools, knowledge, and attitude, we can achieve financial stability, security, and freedom. Financial recovery is not an easy process, but with dedication and hard work, it is possible to achieve our goals and improve our financial health.

By following the advice and steps outlined in this book, you are setting yourself up for a brighter financial future. You now have the knowledge and tools to make informed decisions about your money, create healthy financial habits, and achieve your financial goals. Imagine a future where you are in control of your finances and have the freedom to pursue your passions and dreams. You can travel the world, start your own business, buy your dream home, or retire comfortably. The possibilities are endless when you have a strong financial foundation.

We encourage you to take the first step towards your best future by implementing the strategies and steps outlined in this book. Remember, the key to financial success is consistency, patience, and a willingness to learn and grow. With dedication and perseverance, you can achieve your financial goals and live the life of your dreams. Thank you for joining us on this journey, and I hope that this book has provided you with valuable insights, inspiration, and practical tips for your own financial recovery. Always remember to believe in yourself, stay focused on your goals, and celebrate your progress along the way. Wish you the best on your journey to financial success!

C.H.O.I.C.E. MAP REFLECTION QUESTIONS

Clarify:

What are your goals and priorities for this decision?

Why is this decision important to you?

What outcomes do you hope to achieve?

Hone in:

What are your options and alternatives?

Are there any other choices that you have not considered?

How can you gather more information about each option?

Observe:

What are the pros and cons of each choice?

What are the potential benefits and drawbacks of each option?

How do each option align with your goals and priorities?

Identify:

Which option best aligns with your values and criteria?

How can you prioritize and weigh each factor?

What trade-offs are you willing to make?

Celebrate:

What is the best choice for you based on your evaluation?

What action do you need to take to move forward with your decision?

Are there any potential obstacles or challenges to consider?

Evaluate:

What was the outcome of your decision?

Did your decision align with your goals and priorities?

What did you learn from your experience and how can you apply this to future decisions?

CHALLENGE:

This or That

Chapter 6
Financial Challenge: THIS or THAT

Welcome to Chapter 6 of Tough Financial Choices, where we will be discussing the This or That challenge. If you've been following along with our book so far, you may have already started to think about some of the financial goals you want to achieve. In this chapter, we're going to present a challenge to help you get started on the path towards those goals.

The This or That challenge is all about making small, incremental changes to your daily routines and choices that will add up over time to help you achieve your financial goals. It's based on the idea that even the smallest changes can make a big difference when done consistently over a long period of time.

Here's how the This or That challenge works: first, you need to identify your financial goal. It could be anything from paying off a credit card to saving up for a down payment on a house. Once you have your goal in mind, the next step is to break it down into smaller, more manageable increments. For example, if your goal is to save $10,000 for a down payment, you could break it down into saving $1000 per month for 10 months.

The next step is to start making small changes to your daily routine that will help you achieve that incremental goal. For example, if you're used to eating out for lunch every day, you could start packing your lunch instead and put the money you save towards your goal. If you're used to buying coffee from a coffee shop, you could start making your own coffee at home and put the money you save towards your goal.

The key is to be consistent with these changes over time. It's not about making one big change and expecting everything to magically fall into place. It's about making small, sustainable changes that you can stick to over the long term. Now the most important part is to make sure that throughout the day you are adding up those incremental savings and moving it to a saving account you do not intend on touching. At the end of the day if you have managed to make tough choices leading you to have saved $50 dollars, that money is transferred out so when your goal is met there isn't any confusion and can feel guilt free.

Here are some other examples of small changes you can make that will add up over time:

- ❖ Canceling a subscription you don't use and putting the money you save toward your goal.
- ❖ Switching to a cheaper cell phone plan and putting the money you save towards your goal.
- ❖ Turning off lights and appliances when you're not using them to save on your electricity bill.
- ❖ Shopping around for better deals on your insurance policies and putting the money you save towards your goal.
- ❖ The possibilities are endless, and the key is to find small changes that work for you and your lifestyle.

Now, we know that making these changes may not be easy at first. It can be difficult to break old habits and make new ones. That's why we're presenting this as a challenge to you. We challenge you to identify one small change you can make in your daily routine that will help you achieve your financial goal. Commit to making that change every day for the next month and see how much progress you can make towards your goal.

Remember, the This or That challenge is not about perfection. It's about progress. It's about taking small steps towards your goal every day and celebrating the progress you make along the way.

In conclusion, the This or That challenge is a powerful tool for achieving your financial goals. By making small, sustainable changes to your daily routine, you can make big progress over time. We challenge you to take on the This or That challenge and see how much progress you can make towards your financial goals.

TOUGH *Financial* CHOICES

YOU ARE IN CONTROL

"Tough Financial Choices" is your transformative workbook for empowered decision-making on the path to financial success. With thought-provoking exercises, practical tools, and engaging activities, this guide helps you confront debt, set goals, and make informed choices aligned with your values. Our unique "This or That" challenge presents hypothetical scenarios, guiding you to make tough choices and explore trade-offs. Take control of your financial destiny and embark on a brighter future.

OZZIE **TORRES**
STEPHANIE **TORRES**

Ozzie & Stephanie are husband and wife business partners who dream big with everything they've got. After overcoming their own financial challenges and building their careers as licensed Realtors, Steph & Ozzie started Contigo Real Estate. Contigo, which means "with you" in Spanish, is a place where they can come alongside both clients and agents to help them reach their goals. This book was written out of a desire to walk others through making the tough financial choices that shape their future.

TikTok | Instagram | YouTube
@toughfinancialchoices
toughfinancialchoices@gmail.com

www.ContigoRealEstate.com

www.ingramcontent.com/pod-product-compliance
Lightning Source LLC
Chambersburg PA
CBHW071516220526
45472CB00003B/1051